From Buildings to Bluescapes

Shaping the Future of Urban Agriculture

Table of Contents

Chapter 1. Introduction

In this special report, "From Buildings to Bluescapes: Shaping the Future of Urban Agriculture," we delve into the depths of an astonishing revolution that is transforming our metropolises in breath-taking ways. Much more than just urban farming, this is a story brewed with splendid innovations, visionaries, and the promise of sustainable, health-conscious cities. This report is not laden with technical jargon, but an inspiring, vivid, and accessible journey into an urban landscape where sleek skyscrapers coexist with luxurious lettuce, and bluescapes replace blandscapes. We're thrilled to share insights that will not only enthrall you but may also provoke thoughts on how you can contribute to this remarkable evolution. So, are you ready for a heartening read that paints a vision of tomorrow, right today? Step into the world of urban agriculture and view your city in a light you never imagined before; let's sow some seeds of thought together!

Chapter 2. The Rise of the Urban Jungle

There's a palpable change in the air; it smells of damp earth and tastes of fresh produce. Cities, long viewed as concrete jungles, are transforming into surprising havens of vibrant greenery. This is the tale of humanity's ingenuity turning seemingly sterile buildings into flourishing farms that form the very skeleton of our emergent urban jungles.

2.1. The Dawn of a New Era

The birth of urban agriculture is as much a return to nature as it is a stride into the future. In the face of rapidly decreasing rural spaces and expanding city limits, humanity needed a solution, a path to sustainability that would provide the world's booming population with locally-sourced, nutritious food.

It was more than a responsibility; it was an inevitability. Thus, from the heart of our cities' concrete belly, burgeoned a dream-turned-reality. Rooftops and parking lots became fertile fields, the sterile grey of urban blight made way for an explosion of green. We began to grow upwards, our greenhouses reaching for the skies, breathing life into the harsh city lines and casting verdant hues onto the uniform grey.

2.2. The Technology that Facilitated the Rise

As with any great leap forward, technology provided the ladders for our climb. Hydroponics, a technique that cultivates plants without soil, instead using nutrient-filled water, drastically reduced the weight of our suburban farms, making them viable atop skyscrapers. Aeroponics, a method that involves misting the plants' roots with nutrients, further decreased the mass and even the need for water by up to 90%.

Innovation didn't stop at cultivation techniques. Technologies like LED growth lights, which can be tuned to emit light at the optimal frequencies for plant growth, allowed farms to be built in basements, former factories or even old subway tunnels. Each day saw a new invention, a new step forward, solidifying the rise of the urban jungle.

2.3. How Cities Embraced the Change

City dwellers were quick to embrace the urban farming revolution. The aesthetic appeal of green spaces in a grey metropolis was only the initial charm. The promise of fresh, locally grown food, in contrast to the nutrient-deficient produce transported over thousands of miles, truly won the hearts of urbanites.

Individuals and communities started to transform every available space into potential cropland. Community gardens, sprouting from abandoned plots and railway tracks, turned into common meeting spaces, reinforcing the social fabric of the communities. Convivial gatherings were centered around eating seasonal fruits and vegetables straight from the community garden, a novelty that never ceased to astound.

2.4. The Ecosystem of Urban Agriculture

Urban agriculture seamlessly integrates with city life, creating an ecosystem of its own. The symbiotic relationship evolved further, inducing a shift in behavioral patterns of city dwellers and urban planning. The flora and foliage began to provide insulation to buildings, significantly slashing electricity costs. The greenery absorbed noise and air pollutants, making cities healthier, more livable.

2.4.1. Bees, Birds and the Buzz in the Urban Jungle

Nature quickly caught up with this revolution. The green rooftops and lush gardens drew bees and birds back to cities, critical components of an environment's health. City dwellers once again started waking up to soft bird melodies instead of blaring horns, an epitome of urban-rural harmony.

The food source that urban spaces provided invited a variety of insects, beneficial for both the city and its agriculture. Compost from food and plant waste encouraged fertile soils and reduced the dependency on artificial fertilizers, ensuring the sustainability of urban agriculture.

Urban jungles have emerged. Each day, they grow heftier, favoring the symbiosis of urban living and agricultural practices. Each building is a potential farm. Each city, a future orchard.

Chapter 3. Architects of Change: Visionaries of Urban Agriculture

Visionaries fuel the fire of progress, and in the realm of urban agriculture, this is particularly true. Profound shifts need imaginative minds who can wander beyond the regular path, encapsulating the potential of today's technology and accommodating the needs of both the environment and urban populace. Let's forge ahead and introduce some of these extraordinary pioneers, who are redefining the boundaries of possibility in the urban landscape.

3.1. The Agritech Innovators

Dominating the front line of urban agricultural revolution are the agritech innovators; firms such as AeroFarms, Bowery Farming, and GreenSpirit Farms serve as potent examples. With hydroponic systems, vertical farming, and LED light technology to enhance crop growth, they transform once empty warehouses and buildings into productive havens for fresh produce.

AeroFarms, a pioneer in aeroponics, creates farms with multilayered, vertical stacks. They utilize a mist environment, reducing water usage by up to 95%. Bowery Farming expands on this approach with its proprietary technology, BoweryOS, responsible for automating, monitoring, and trimming crop growth. GreenSpirit Farms, on the other hand, ventures into abandoned spaces in cities, converting them into thriving indoor farms.

These innovative forays demonstrate the significance of technology in producing food that's sustainable, local, and resilient against weather conditions. With these advancements, our metropolises are becoming fields for not only business and industry but also for food growth– a landscape that few could have imagined a century ago.

3.2. The Architects of Abundance

Taking the reins from agritech innovators are the urban designers and urban planners – the architects who envision landscapes filled with greenery. They amalgamate the aesthetics with the functional, transforming rooftops, balconies, and unused urban spaces into vibrant greenscapes.

One notable figure is Dickson Despommier, the proponent of the "Vertical Farm" concept. His idea of transforming skyscrapers into vertical farms, thereby creating spaces that are engaging and productive, takes urban farming to new heights. Then there's Kate Orff, founder of SCAPE, using 'oyster-tecture' to purify water and support seafood production in cities.

These visionaries are reshaping our cities into living, breathing organisms that nurture us just as we nurture them. As urban spaces become less concrete and more green, they foster psychological benefits and enhance community engagement.

3.3. The Policy Pioneers

The evolution of urban agriculture would be incomplete without the mention of the policy pioneers. These are the city leaders, policymakers, and NGOs who understand the importance of legislative support for urban farming. Their decisions can promote or halt the progress of urban agriculture, depending on the funding, zoning laws, and legislation they implement.

A shining example is the city of Detroit, where the local government has ardently supported urban farming. Their 'Urban Agriculture Ordinance' has enabled Detroit to transform from being an industrial giant to a prototype of 21st-century urban agriculture. Other cities, like New York and Chicago, are also following suit and incorporating policies that foster urban farming.

3.4. The Entrepreneur Enablers

Finally, companies and individuals who bridge the gap between traditional marketplaces and urban farms also play a substantial role. Platforms like FreshDirect, a popular online grocery delivery service, have incorporated Urban Produce sections, hosting crops from local urban farms. Another notable entrant is Blue Apron, which sources organic food from urban farms and delivers them to clients with an easy-to-make recipe.

Through these initiatives, urban agriculture is no longer an alien concept to city dwellers. It is woven into their daily lives, enticing them to support these practices.

The future of our cities rests on the shoulders of these visionaries – the innovators, designers, policymakers, and enablers. Their relentless endeavors collectively shape the prospects of urban agriculture, making our cities sustainable, while providing local, fresh, and healthy food.

Indeed, the future starts in our cities – at the intersection of necessity and innovation where urban agriculture proliferates. As we proceed into the 21st century, it is these characters of change who will determine the shape of our urban existence. And at this juncture, that shape is looking greener than ever. Through urban agriculture, we witness a shift in both consciousness and landscape, birthing bluescapes where grey once dominated. The astonishing revolution continues, setting an exciting precedent for urban design and ecological consciousness.

Chapter 4. Harvesting Skyscrapers: Vertical Farming

Let's turn our gaze upwards to our city skylines. Many see an expanse of concrete and glass, reaching for the sky in a testament to mankind's prowess. But, do we see the same? Can we visualize these towering structures, not just with glass-panelled offices and swanky penthouses, but also verdant with layers of green, abundant with succulent fruits and vegetables? That's the vision of vertical farming – turning our cities into abundant food hubs.

4.1. The Concept and Benefits

Vertical farming is an innovative method of urban agriculture that uses vertical space to cultivate plants, effectively 'harvesting' skyscrapers. The idea is so challenging as it is fascinating: growing produce in stacked vertical layers, usually inside urban buildings either under artificial lights or in combination with natural light.

Vertical farming has multiple benefits that can help shape sustainable urban life in the future:

- **Resource Efficiency:** By stacking multiple layers of plants on top of each other, vertical farms can produce significantly more food per square foot than conventional farming.

- **Localized Food Production:** It brings production closer to consumers, reducing the carbon footprint associated with long-haul transportation of food.

- **Year-round Cultivation:** Climate-controlled environments mean cultivation can happen year-round, independent of weather conditions.

- **Effective Use of Urban Space:** Vertical farming utilizes existing urban buildings to contribute to city-wide sustainability efforts.

These advantages make harvesting skyscrapers a pivotal point in the future of urban agriculture.

4.2. The Science Inside The Skyscraper

While it sounds simple, vertical farming is a marriage of biology and technology, powered by advancements in various fields from crop science to data analytics. For instance, plants are often grown hydroponically, without soil, drenching their roots directly in nutrient-rich water solutions.

Artificial light comes into play in most vertical farming setups. Light Emitting Diodes (LEDs) optimize the spectrum of light for plant growth, promoting faster and healthier output. While sunlight is the ideal source of light energy, LEDs allow for the continuous cultivation of crops within the confines of a skyscraper.

Sensors and algorithms form another essential part of vertical farming, monitoring conditions like temperature, humidity, and light levels, ensuring optimal growing conditions, and adjusting them when needed. This kind of precision agriculture allows for minimal water and energy waste.

4.3. Image of the Future

Envision a skyscraper turned into a lush vertical farm. Each floor thrums with life, filled with rows upon rows of vegetables, herbs, and fruits. The sound of water dripping in the background from hydroponic systems lends a calming ambiance. LED lights bathe plants in vibrant colors that encourage growth.

Outside, the edifice is alive, seemingly draped in a tapestry of foliage. Rooftop greenhouses accentuate the building further, making it stand out as a beacon calling out to a period where cities coexist with their ecosystem rather than dominate it.

This 'green-beacon' concept art of the future conveys a message: Harvesting skyscrapers will not just grow vegetables; it will foster a connection between city-dwellers and their food, making agriculture an integrated part of urban life, not just a remote occupation.

4.4. Emerging

Vertical farming is no longer a fantasy. From New York to Singapore, urban vertical farms are sprouting, transforming bleak concrete into dynamic greenscapes.

In Tokyo, 'Pasona O2' is an underground vertical farm illuminating a subterranean vault with a spectacular array of crops. Closer to home, you might have heard of 'AeroFarms' in New Jersey, an indoor farm that grows its leafy greens using aeroponic systems – a method that requires no soil and significantly less water than traditional methods.

These spaces not only provide nutritious, local food but also contribute to cities' sustainability efforts. They bring people closer to the food they eat and invite them to understand agriculture's importance in a very direct and personal way.

So, vertical farming is not just agriculture. It's nurturing verdant ecosystems within concrete jungles. It's a giant leap towards sustainable urban living, a testament to human ingenuity, and a celebration of agriculture's harmonious integration into city skylines.

4.5. From Theory to Practice

Now that we have painted the picture of vertical farming and its potential virtues, the task is operationalizing it. The biggest challenges of vertical farming are cost and energy consumption. High-tech systems such as LEDs and hydroponic systems, while efficient, could be pricey to install and consume a significant amount of electricity.

However, advances in technology — more efficient LED lights, renewable energy sources, more cost-effective building materials, and the constant innovation in hydroponic and aeroponic technologies — are bringing us closer to cost-effective vertical farming.

We also need to consider societal acceptance. Consumers may need time to adjust to the idea of eating crops grown in a city skyscraper. Education and engagement will be key to encouraging consumption of locally produced, vertical-farmed produce.

Harvesting skyscrapers presents a fresh perspective on urban agricultural practices. It's not just an efficient farming technique; it's an ethos promoting sustainable and local food systems in an entirely novel and inspirational way. The view of our city skylines might change soon, replaced by lush green towers. As we peer into the future, let's remember: When we aim for the sky, why stop at rooftops? Let's go beyond to the limitless possibilities that vertical farming presents.

Our cities stand at the precipice of a bold step towards a greener future. With vertical farming, we're not just harvesting crops; we're harvesting hope for sustainable, self-sufficient metropolises of tomorrow.

Chapter 5. Grey to Green: Transforming Concrete to Cropland

Cities, identified by their collection of superstructures, glossy structures of glass, and mazed networks of concrete pathways, are undertaking an unprecedented transformation. A vision is increasingly sprouting, quite literally, from the rooftops to the basements — turning the grey tinge of urban landscapes green.

5.1. The Green Revolution within our Concrete Jungles

The concept of urban jungles is not new. But what does it traditionally bring to mind? Towering edifices, honking cars, and huddled masses? Certainly. Rows of thriving vegetable gardens and orchards painted across the backdrop of sky-blazing office towers? Not so much. But remarkably, this once-odd vision is gradually becoming reality as cities worldwide are intertwining sustainability and innovation to create a flourishing ecosystem within their confines.

The eruption of urban agriculture signifies the dawn of a resounding revolution — one that is breaking down traditional barriers and conceptions of what our cities can truly embody. Major cities globally are committing to the goal of creating more sustainable, resilient, and health-focused communities, and the transformation of concrete to cropland plays a critically important role in realizing these ambitions.

5.2. Sowing Seeds on Concrete: A Tale of Innovation

Take a walk in a concrete jungle and chances are that you might stumble upon a paradise of lush vegetation – a rooftop garden, basement greenhouses, or urban farms on vacant properties. Imaginative utilization of these city spaces has appeared to be a true testament to human ingenuity. Notably, urban agriculture goes beyond merely transforming landscapes and also manifests as an efficient response to the growing challenges of food security, population growth, economic solace, and increasing climate change concerns.

Intriguingly, a New Yorker can now relish salad leaves, straight from rooftop farms like Brooklyn Grange. In Chicago, the South Side district thrives with fresh produce from an array of urban and community gardens. Singapore, a city with minimal land resource for farming, has sprouted sky-high vertical farms. These examples stand as a testament to the scalable potential of urban agriculture, proof that even in hardened city hearts, an oasis of green can voluntarily thrive.

5.3. The Grey-Green Tech-Innovation Intersection

Just as vital as the 'green' in this green revolution is the technology paired with it. Innovators and startups are creating cutting-edge solutions to drive this movement — from robotics and automation in farming practices, AI-backed climate control for maximum yields, to water-conserving irrigation systems. These technologies not only propel urban agriculture to the forefront of sustainable urban development but also significantly improve productivity and reduce environmental impact.

Take, for example, the concept of Aeroponics, a plant-cultivation technique where plants' roots are intermittently sprayed with nutrient-laden water mists, requiring no soil and 90% less water. AeroFarms, a vertical farming company, uses aeroponics to harvest up to 390 times more crops per square foot than traditional farming methods. This demonstration of intersection between technology and sustainable practices paves the way for more wider acceptance and adoption of urban farming.

5.4. Challenges: From Fertile to Firm Ground

Yet, like any nascent movement, urban agriculture has its challenges. Legal obstacles, funding insecurities, and skill gaps can throw the proverbial wrench in the efforts to create city farms. Moreover, the necessary shift in perception from viewing farming as a rural endeavor to an urban one is often slower than desired.

Addressing these issues requires engaged civic participation, feasible policies and regulations that encourage urban farming, and targeted educational initiatives. Ultimately, the sustenance and growth of urban agriculture hang on building an ecosystem that collaboratively addresses these challenges, facilitating this metamorphosis from concrete to cropland.

5.5. The Future is Green: Harvesting Hope

With more people moving to metropolises every day, and cities projected to house 70% of the world's population by 2050, the prospect of greener urban environments is no longer just desirable, but indeed, crucial. The transformation of concrete jungles into thriving green croplands promises a sustainable, viable solution to the myriad of challenges our urban centers face.

Witnessing the change of barren rooftops or unused urban spaces into green oasis is truly a sight to behold. Urban agriculture is not just about growing food. It's much bigger than that. It's about revitalizing communities, revitalizing cities, and revitalizing our connection with the environment – essentially, transforming the grey to green.

So, next time when you sail through the concrete arteries of your bustling city, do take a moment to explore the patches of green around you – perhaps a rooftop verdure, an alleyway full of herbs, or a high-tech vertical farm. Who knows, your next meal could come from a garden grown right in the heart of your city!

Chapter 6. Embracing Tech: Innovations in Urban Farming

Technology has galloped into every sector imaginable, and agriculture is no exception. The dusty boots stereotypically associated with farming have merged with Silicon Valley's slick keyboards, giving rise to an exciting era replete with innovations that are redefining our understanding of urban farming.

6.1. From Soil to Software

Traditional agriculture relies heavily on manual labor and land. The picture of an extensive open field dotted with corn rows or sparkled by the occasional sunflower isn't just romantic; it's an integrated part of our global vision of agriculture. However, urban farming is challenging this narrative, powered by groundbreaking technology.

Software plays a crucial role in modern urban agriculture. Precision farming tools deliver insights on crop health, temperature, humidity, light, and other parameters that determine growth. Digital platforms serve as an interface for urban farmers to access this critical information, enabling decisions based on real-time and historical data.

Smart technology also empowers farmers to monitor and control farming environments remotely. Internet of Things (IoT) connected sensors and devices can communicate, interpret data, and even act on the resulting insights. Consequently, optimal conditions are maintained, minimizing waste, running costs, and boosting productivity in ways traditional farming could never have managed.

IoT-powered urban farms can go a long way in addressing the food shortages projected by ongoing urbanization and population explosion. Equipped with smart tech, urban farmers are also better poised to deal with climate change challenges since they control their farming environment.

6.2. Aquaponics: Balancing Ecosystems in the Concrete Jungle

Aquaponics, another technology-enabled approach, combines aquaculture and hydroponics. While hydroponics is soil-less farming, aquaculture involves raising aquatic creatures. In this system, the fish waste serves as organic food for the plants, and the plants naturally filter the water in which the fish live. Essentially, it's a mini ecosystem contained within a metropolitan setting.

Beyond the symbiotic relationship between the fish and plants, aquaponics leverages tech to regulate and optimize conditions vital for mutual survival. pH, temperature, ammonia levels, nitrites, and nitrates are tracked assiduously. Automated systems respond to these parameters, adjusting conditions accordingly to ensure longevity and, in turn, productivity.

Not only is aquaponics incredibly efficient, but it is also significantly eco-friendly. It scarcely uses any soil and requires about 90% less water than traditional farming per unit of output, making it a beacon of sustainable agriculture.

6.3. Vertical Farming: Towards a Greener Skyline

More than just a novelty, vertical farming represents a seismic shift in urban agriculture. Floor upon floor, shelves stacked with leafy greens tower upward, driven by the ambition to unlock the full potential of our limited urban spaces.

Central to this approach are LED lights, which have experienced drastic improvements over the past decade. LEDs emit specific light spectrums, such as red and blue, essential for photosynthesis. Coupled with their energy efficiency and long-life span, they have become indispensable in vertical farming.

These farms also deploy climate-controlled systems and automated watering mechanisms. An important spin-off of this controlled environment is that vertical farms can produce crops year-round and are less susceptible to weather vagaries, pests, and diseases. The result? A persistent supply of fresh and safe food for urban dwellers.

Lastly, vertical farms invoke the notion of localization. This means produce is grown within city limits, reducing the resources expended on long-distance transportation and refrigeration.

6.4. Drones and Robots: An Unusual Farmhand

A new age beckons on the horizon of urban farming with the introduction of farming robots and drones. These machines reduce the labor required while increasing accuracy, efficiency, and output.

Drones, equipped with multispectral imaging sensors, are used to monitor plant health, pest infestations, nutrient deficiencies, and more. They capture detailed aerial images that are processed to provide valuable feedback.

Robots too are proving invaluable. Crop-harvesting robots, for instance, are designed to select and pick ripe produce with speed and precision. On one hand, they save time and reduce labor costs. On the other, they help to mitigate food loss and waste caused by inadequate, hasty, or improper harvests.

Self-driving tractors, robotic weeders, and autonomous planters are also part of this innovative league, redefining what 'hands-on farming' means in an urban context.

Interestingly, the advent of machine learning and artificial intelligence (AI) has amplified the advantages of these technologies. AI provides predictive analytics that help in making informed decisions on when to plant, water, fertilize, and harvest, transforming agriculture into a predictive rather than reactive endeavor.

6.5. The Future is Here

Technology's influence on urban farming cannot be understated. It facilitates the leap from traditional fields to high-tech farms, no longer confined to rural expanses but nestled right in our cityscapes.

From vast software applications, aquaponics systems, towering vertical farms, to the tireless work of drones and robots, the marriage of agriculture and technology represents a vital step toward sustainable, efficient, and healthful food production.

As cities continue to swell and climate change darkens the horizon, these innovations in urban farming shine bright, providing us with a sure path to follow and the promise of a future where technology and nature walk hand in hand, feeding the world in a truly revolutionary way. So let us welcome this era of technological transformation, as the concrete jungles bloom into bountiful bluescapes.

Chapter 7. Feeding Future Cities: Sustainability and Food Security

As the sun rises over our bustling metropolises, the dawn of a new era in food production and consumption is upon us. An era where each city becomes a self-sustaining bedrock of fresh, nutritious, and vibrant fruits and vegetables—a prospect once imagined as part of some utopian dream, now firmly cementing its roots in our urban reality. With escalating demands spurred by growing populations and the urgent necessity to reinforce sustainability, urban-agricultural ventures are our tickets to securing our cities' – and by extension, the world's – future.

7.1. An Overview: The Urban Agriculture Revolution

You might not see it from your office window, but there's a revolution unfurling on your city's rooftops, in vacant lots, and even nestled between towering skyscrapers. Urban agriculture is taking hold, a movement that mobilizes city-dwellers and rural farmers alike, championed by a desire for food security, sustainability, and community resilience.

Urban farms are not merely an emblem of innovation—they are functional realms of growth that challenge conventional exclusivity of food production to rural geography. Sprawling over rooftops, balconies, and vacant lands, these urban farms are productive spaces injecting green life into our concrete jungles. They displace the antiquated one-way flow from rural to urban, bringing food production to the doorstep of consumers, or better yet, inspiring cities dwellers to become producers themselves.

7.2. Harvesting Benefits: Sustainability and Beyond

Urban agriculture's potential goes beyond just beautifying cities or providing a fresh aesthetic. This evolution promises a plethora of benefits that will reshape our cities— from a sustainable standpoint, yes, but from an economical, communal, and health perspective too.

For starters, urban farming significantly reduces the need for transportation of produce from rural farms to city markets, thereby shrinking carbon footprints. Moreover, it utilizes and converts vacant land or degraded areas into lush, productive landscapes. Urban farming promotes biodiversity, generates employment, and presents a localized solution to food security challenges.

From a more community-centric viewpoint, urban agriculture can foster a sense of belonging. Community farms make for great spaces where people can partake in growth—it doesn't require much stretch of imagination to see these places as classrooms without walls, where cities' inhabitants partake in sowing, tending, and reaping, breaking down barriers of isolation and nurturing bonds through shared culture of cultivation.

7.3. Food Security: A Step Towards Self-Sufficiency

Food security, a term which gained prevalence in the 20th century, is essentially access to safe, nutritious, and culturally acceptable food for all, at all times. Clearly, the relevance of food security has shot up multiple folds in a world undergoing rapid urbanization, bringing unique challenges to the table.

Urban agriculture might just be the bold solution we need. It brings food production closer to consumption, shrinks dependency on lengthy supply chains, and puts control back into the hands of the city dwellers. Community farms ensure that fresh produce is accessible and affordable to consumers across income strata. Moreover, cities can reduce their dependence on food imports and broaden the range of available food varieties. Keeping citizens fed, fostering local economic growth, and injecting resilience into food systems, urban agriculture is undoubtedly feeding our future cities.

7.4. The Role of Technology: Turning Science into Sustenance

The rise in urban agriculture owes a great deal to technological advancements. Hydroponic systems, vertical farming, and precision agriculture, among other technologies, have transformed previously unused urban spaces into productive agricultural hubs.

Vertical farming, with its stacked layers of cultivation, is akin to having multiple mini-farms functioning within one urban unit. This innovative approach boosts productivity, requires less water than traditional farming, and can function all year round, making fresh produce accessible regardless of seasonal changes.

Likewise, hydroponic systems, which rely on nutrient-rich water rather than soil, exemplify the capability to expand farming possibilities beyond traditional confines. They can be installed in numerous urban settings, from rooftops to basements, creating an array of micro-environments where a variety of produce can thrive. This futuristic approach to farming liberates us from sole dependence on fertile land for food production, bringing it into our concrete enclaves and putting food production in our own hands.

Whether through vertical farms that sprout amidst our cityscapes or community gardens that foster unity, the future of urban agriculture is undoubtedly bright. By bridging the rural-urban gap in food production, these gardens of growth hold the key to more resilient, sustainable and self-sustaining cities.

7.5. The Way Forward: Shaping Tomorrow's Cities

For all its potential, urban agriculture should not be perceived as a one-size-fits-all solution to our food security and sustainability challenges. Instead, it is a powerful component in a much larger, complex tapestry that weaves in traditional agriculture, supply-chain dynamics, political will, access to resources, and societal support.

Integration of urban farming into municipalities' strategic vision can shape our cities' future. Policies that encourage the conversion of vacant urban spaces into farmland, endorse the use of public spaces for community gardens, and provide appropriate support and resources for these initiatives are just a few of the steps required to weave urban farming into the fabric of our cities.

That said, our role as individuals is equally, if not more important. By participating in community gardens, supporting local urban farms, or even setting up a vertical garden in our own homes, we can inject momentum into this movement.

Through the evolution of our cities into producers, we are on the brink of shaping a new chapter in the narrative of human development. The current momentum propelling the urban agriculture movement, coupled with initiative from local governments and communities, can trailblaze a future where nourishment is not just about the food we eat but also the cities we inhabit. As we stand face to face with the dawn of this revolution, every seed of change we sow resonates with the rhythm of growth. Feeding our future cities starts with us, our decisions, and our actions today.

Chapter 8. Blossoms Amidst Bricks: Cultivating Green Communities

Urban transformations aren't new but bringing agriculture into city centers and integrating it into the urban texture is something of a revolution and unarguably, the phenomenon of our era. The concrete jungle is going green, and the change is well underway. No longer are city streets just a vast maze of buildings, it's now becoming common to see gardens suspended in the sky, sprouting from balconies, flourishing on rooftops, wedged in alleyways, and even thriving above subway systems. There's a deliberate focus to infuse the urban gray with bits of green. Welcome to an audacious green revolution; welcome to the era of green communities.

8.1. A Rainbow Rises

Every green endeavor begins with a seed, the promise of life. The seeds of this revolution were sown, ironically, amidst the concrete, bricks, and glass. It all began with a need to enhance our quality of living, to breathe fresh, unpolluted air, to eat fresh, chemical-free produce. These underlying needs spurred communities to reimagine the urban landscape from a utilitarian perspective, to maximize the use of land, water, and energy efficiently while reducing waste. Be it growing food on rooftops, upcycling waste products into planters, or creating community gardens within city blocks, urban dwellers are redefining what one can expect from a typical city scene.

Take the example of Singapore, famously known as the 'Garden City,' where the government has set a goal to produce 30% of its nutritional needs locally by 2030. Singapore's sky farm, a 9,000 m2 rooftop farm on one of their high-rise buildings, is an inspiration globally. It has not only taken the concept of self-sustenance to new heights but also contributed to reducing the island city's reliance on imported food.

8.2. Green Communities: More Than Just a Garden

Urban farming isn't only about turning vacant spaces into productive ones. It's about creating spaces where community members can come together to learn, share knowledge, rejuvenate, and connect with nature. Green communities are social ecosystems that unite people under an environmental cause.

In Berlin, Prinzessinnengarten, a vacant plot turned urban garden, is one such example of how urban farming can stimulate social and cultural life. This urban farm is a gathering spot, hosting workshops on organic farming, and serving as an open-air classroom for children to learn about ecology and conservation.

8.3. Technology Driving Urban Greenery

Technology plays a significant role in advancing urban agriculture and shaping green communities. Innovations such as LED lights that simulate sunlight, modular hydroponic systems, and vertical farming are driving a new era of urban agriculture that is both scalable and sustainable.

In Tokyo, Pasona Group, a recruiting company, has made a bold statement by converting their nine-story headquarters into an urban farm. Employing hydroponic and aeroponic technologies besides traditional soil-based farming, this vertical farm yields over 200 types of plants, including rice, tomatoes, and strawberries. It is a testament to incorporating greenery into cityscapes, linking the urban work-life with rural farming roots.

8.4. Responding to the Challenges

Like any revolution, the rise of green communities has not been without its challenges, from lingering misconceptions about aesthetics to structural requirements for rooftop gardens. However, the resilience of these communities has led to creative solutions. For instance, green roofs often employ lightweight, highly absorbent materials that enable plant growth without a high load on the building. These solutions are indicative of the sheer determination and creativity of city dwellers committed to nurturing green spaces within their urban landscapes.

8.5. Closing Thoughts

Urban landscapes are changing, and the blossoms amidst bricks serve as a ray of hope for the future. As we pave the way to coexist with nature in high-rises, train stations, and houses, we continue to more closely align our practices with an understanding of the natural world and the way it works. The dream of green communities may be budding now, but the future holds a lush bloom for our cities. The revolution is here, and it's green. Welcome to tomorrow.

Chapter 9. Lessons from the Past: Historical Context of Urban Agriculture

As we wade deeper into the journey of urban agriculture, it's essential to remember that every phenomenon has its roots and previous iterations which shape its present and guide its future. Urban agriculture is not a novelty of the 21st Century; it's an evolution of practices stretching back hundreds, even thousands, of years.

9.1. From Field to Cityscape

The first evidence of urban farming finds roots in the ancient civilizations of Egypt, Mesopotamia, and the Indus Valley around 3500 BC. These civilizations employed canal irrigation systems for controlling water flow for their crops, nestled in and around their urban dwellings. Each subsequent civilization, showing an even tighter integration of farming within city walls, further evolved this practice.

Fast forward to the Middle Ages in Europe, and we find gardens were a staple element in monasteries. Monastic gardens incorporated space for medicines, vegetables, and flowers within their compound. These provided for the monastic community and extended to support the local populace. The concept of allotments, small portions of land for personal cultivation, also emerged during this era, evolving into the urban community gardens we see today.

9.2. From World Wars to Rooftop Gardens

The 20th Century saw significant expansion in urban agriculture across the globe, especially during periods of war and subsequent economic depressions. Victory gardens emerged during World War I and II as a means to supplement food supplies, reduce pressure on the public food supply, and boost public morale. These gardens speckled rooftops, vacant lots, backyards, and public lands, painting a dramatic landscape of city-dwellers turned warriors of sustenance.

During the 1930s, the Great Depression bolstered the appeal of Relief Gardens in the United States, providing a vital lifeline for households impacted by rampant unemployment. Similarly, Cuba's government embraced urban agriculture in the 1990s during their "Periodo Especial," an economic crisis following the dissolution of the Soviet Union, which cut off their imports of chemical fertilizers and pesticides. The necessity fostered an organic movement that persists today.

9.3. Urban Agriculture in the Postwar Period

After World War II, urban agriculture saw a gradual decline in the developed world, swept away by increasing urbanisation and the spread of supermarkets. In developing countries, however, it continued as a crucial survival strategy and a significant contributor to the urban food supply, particularly in Africa, Latin America, and Asia.

Despite being frowned upon by city planners and authorities due to concerns about zoonotic diseases, urban vegetable systems have continuously fed booming urban populations — sometimes providing up to 90% of the urban supply of perishable vegetables.

9.4. Post-1970s: The Rise of Community Gardens

The movement against the establishment, coupled with an environmental awakening in the 1970s, rekindled the allure of urban agriculture among city populations. A push towards self-reliance and a way to beautify derelict lots, coupled with the alternative food movement's birth, positioned urban agriculture under conservation policies. Community gardens thrived, increasing in number and hectares over successive decades, transforming into urban farms contributing to local fresh food baskets.

9.5. Modern Times: Tech-Integrated Urban Agriculture

With technological advancements in the 21st Century, from hydroponics to rooftop gardens, urban agriculture has become synonymous with sustainability and climate-smart cities. It appeals to city-dwellers' desire to have a deeper connection with their food sources and contributes positively to the local economy.

Today, Urban agriculture is practiced in various modern metropoles like Detroit, Vancouver, and Singapore, where cityscape and foodscapes merge, creating a revolution that is distinctly urban yet passionately pastoral.

As we explore the recent trends and possibilities in urban agriculture, each step is informed by these past learnings. Witnessing these historical advancements, one can't help but marvel at the persistent human endeavour to harness the Earth's bounties, even within the concrete jungle of cities.

Chapter 10. The Economic Impact of the Green Movement

Urban agriculture, and especially the rise of vertical and rooftop farming, is impacting our cities in profound and unexpected ways. Not only is it opening up a new world of exciting possibilities for urban dwellers to reconnect with nature, but it is also fostering a sense of community, sparking innovation, and flexing economic muscle.

10.1. The Financial Boon and Job Creation

Urban agriculture presents a new frontier for economic growth while providing food security and environmental sustainability. This greening initiative is bolstering job creation, for instance, the urban farm industry has created an estimated 33 full-time jobs per acre in the U.S., according to the Agriculture Department reports.

Moreover, it's not just traditional farming work that these ventures are providing. With the infusion of technology into agriculture, a whole host of new tech-based jobs are cropping up, spanning from farm system engineers to IoT solutions developers. Additionally, this green movement has ignited new retail, services, and manufacturing industries, such as the creation of rooftop greenhouse kits and indoor gardening equipment, contributing to the local economy and creating new income streams.

10.2. Investment in Green Economy

Another key aspect to consider is the growth in investments inclined towards the green economy. Astoundingly, green investments are gaining momentum quickly. A report by the FTSE Russell noted a staggering growth in green investing, with nearly $30 billion of net new money placed into green bonds in 2020.

The shift towards urban farming is set to receive a significant part of this funding, with local governments and private investors finding this area more attractive due to the wide range of benefits it provides. Sectors like real estate are also witnessing a gratifying trend. Green buildings not only carry a premium value but also show lower vacancy rates as consumers are increasingly factoring sustainability into their purchase decisions.

10.3. Impact on Traditional Agriculture and Supply Chain

Interestingly, the trend of urban farming is also influencing traditional agriculture and supply chains. Locally produced foods alleviate the strain on transportation and reduces the carbon footprint, contributing to significant environmental and financial savings. Reduced food mileage, less spoilage, and the possibility of year-round growing thanks to controlled environments are the distinct advantages making urban farming a more appealing investment.

10.4. Health, Nutrition & Consumer Willingness to Pay More

Urban agriculture's role in providing locally grown, fresh, and nutritious food close to the consumers is also leading to changes in purchasing behavior. According to a report by Nielsen, an increasing number of consumers, approximately 66%, are willing to pay more for sustainable brands. Urban farming effectively combines the desire for sustainability and health, deeply connecting with consumers' preferences.

Moreover, the unprecedented global focus on health and wellness due to the COVID-19 pandemic has further promoted the demand for local, fresh, and nutritious food, triggering an uptick in the economic impact of urban agriculture.

10.5. The Road to Resilience

Urban agriculture ventures stand out as effective tools for urban resilience. Cities with robust urban agriculture capabilities have the added advantage of food security in times of crises. This factor adds an economic value that is more than mere money; it makes cities self-sufficient and crisis-resistant.

Apart from these, the green movement has an immense social impact. It creates inclusive urban spaces, successfully reduces food deserts, contributes to bettering mental wellbeing, and fosters a sense of community among urban dwellers. These factors are destined to bring about a heightened connection to and emphasis on locally sustainable practices, reinforcing the economic success of the green movement.

In conclusion, the economic impact of the green movement in cities is multi-faceted and influential. Whether it's in catalyzing job creation, attracting investments, revolutionizing supply chains, or encouraging health-conscious consumption, urban agriculture is infusing a bullish sentiment in the green economy. The movement underscores the fact that sustainability and economic stability are not disparate entities; they can synchronize harmoniously to foster healthier, vibrant, and resilient cities. For city planners and stakeholders, embracing the green revolution is not just desirable, but increasingly, it's becoming a necessity. The seeds of a green economic revolution have indeed been sown in the heart of our urban landscapes, and it's just the beginning.

Chapter 11. Blazing Forward: The Next Steps for Urban Agriculture

Urban agriculture, once a fringe movement for green-thumb city dwellers, has recently emerged to attract global attention thanks to its multi-faceted potential to address several key concerns of our day: food security, environmental sustainability, and the re-envisioning of urban landscapes. As we stand on the cusp of a new era, we explore the bold footsteps charting the path forward for urban agriculture. Venture into a world of rooftop farms, high-tech vertical agriculture, city-based CSAs, and more as we detail the transformative steps that trailblazers in the field are taking.

11.1. The Leap from Traditional to High-tech

At the confluence of technology and agriculture, urban farming is being reborn. Rather than simply transplanting the archetypal farm into an urban environment, innovators are increasingly leveraging advanced technologies to maximize outputs and minimize inputs – land, water, energy, and even time.

Traditional hydroponics, which sought to minimize water usage, have evolved into aeroponics, a technique that sprays nutrients directly onto the roots of crops, using up to 98% less water. These technologies, often paired with controlled environment agriculture, allow crops to be grown year-round irrespective of outdoor conditions, virtually anywhere, and with significantly increased yields.

LED technology has also revolutionized urban agriculture. It consumes less energy than traditional grow lamps and can be fine-tuned to the exact spectrum each crop needs for optimal growth. Some urban farms have even deployed AI and machine learning algorithms to monitor plant health and optimize growing conditions – creating intelligent and truly futuristic farming systems.

11.2. Ascent of the Vertical Farm

The urbanization of agriculture often means dealing with an acute scarcity of space. In cities where every inch counts, vertical farming has arisen as an ingenious solution. Stacking layers of crops into vertical structures optimizes the use of available space and opens up new possibilities for food production.

Vertical farming isn't confined to just high-rise towers. It's also being utilized in once vacant structures, transforming disused retail spaces and abandoned buildings into thriving food production centers. These vertical farms, which can produce crops year-round, are stimulating economic growth and addressing food desert issues within their communities.

11.3. Connecting with Communities

CSA programs (Community Supported Agriculture) have been essential in building a bridge between urban agriculture and city residents. They offer a subscription-based model where urban dwellers invest in a share of a local farm's harvest, catalyzing a mutually beneficial relationship.

Presence in farmers' markets and local restaurants further solidifies these connections and fosters relationships that reward both farmers and consumers. Urban farms now contribute to the city's economy, not just by producing fresh produce, but by creating jobs, revitalizing neighborhoods, and facilitating education about sustainable diet choices.

11.4. Turning Skies into Farms

Rooftop farming is another facet of urban agriculture redefining city landscapes. These green havens not only produce food but also reduce urban heat island effects, enhance stormwater management, and provide crucial habitats for urban wildlife.

Rooftop farms, such as those in Montreal and New York, have shown how under-utilized spaces can be transformed into vibrant, productive settings. As urban building codes adapt to accommodate these spaces, we're likely to see rooftop greening efforts increasing.

11.5. The Role of Policy and Planning

The successes of urban agriculture can't be attributed to technology and invention alone. Policies and urban planning play a vital role in enabling this sector to flourish. Governments and institutions worldwide are creating regulatory frameworks to promote and protect urban agricultural initiatives.

Cities such as Detroit and Toronto have integrated urban agriculture into their formal planning documents, and others are following suit. A push for more inclusive zoning laws, tax incentives for green roofs, and funding for public-private partnerships could propel urban agriculture to the forefront of city policy.

11.6. The Future Beckons

The future of urban agriculture is rife with possibilities – from employing cutting-edge technologies to honing community relationships, to shifting public policy and private interests in favor of local, sustainable food production. As we look forward to this promising horizon, let us remember that each of us has a role to play in cultivating this vibrant future, not just for our cities, but for our planet as a whole.

In the words of naturalist and author Wendell Berry, "The Earth is what we all have in common." Urban agriculture, with its potential to bring people, communities, and the natural world closer together, underlines the truth of this sentiment in the most pragmatic way. Therein lies its charm, and therein, its true potential.